REVOLUTIONIZE
YOUR LEADERSHIP

Ammanuel Santa Anna

www.luminousprosperity.com

CONTENTS

TRANSFORMATIVE LEADERSHIP:

Mastering Organizational Change with Appreciative Inquiry and Integral Theory

By Ammanuel Santa Anna

REVOLUTIONIZE YOUR LEADERSHIP

Mastering Appreciative Inquiry and Integral Theory for Unprecedented Corporate Success

By Ammanuel Santa Anna

Table of Contents

Appreciative Inquiry and Integral Theory

Conclusion: The Future of Corporate Transformation with Appreciative Inquiry and Integral Theory

CHAPTER 1: INTRODUCTION TO APPRECIATIVE INQUIRY AND INTEGRAL THEORY IN CORPORATE TRANSFORMATION

Understanding Appreciative Inquiry and Integral Theory

Appreciative Inquiry and Integral Theory are two powerful frameworks that, when combined, create a transformative approach for corporations seeking success in today's dynamic business environment. Appreciative Inquiry focuses on the positive aspects of an organization, seeking to build on its strengths and successes rather than focusing on its weaknesses. Integral Theory, on the other hand, provides a comprehensive and holistic view of an organization, considering all aspects of its operations and culture. When these two frameworks are integrated, they create a powerful tool for corporate executives to drive positive change and achieve sustainable growth.

Appreciative Inquiry and Integral Theory are particularly effective in leadership development, as they provide a deep understanding of an individual's strengths and capabilities. By focusing on what works well within an organization and leveraging these strengths, leaders can inspire and motivate their teams to achieve greater success. This approach not only fosters a positive work culture but also enhances employee morale and engagement, leading to higher levels of productivity and innovation.

Organizational change is a constant in today's fast-paced business world, and Appreciative Inquiry and Integral Theory offer a unique perspective on how to navigate these changes effectively. By encouraging a collaborative and inclusive approach to change management, organizations can ensure that all stakeholders are engaged and committed to the transformation process. This results in smoother transitions, increased buy-in from employees, and ultimately, greater success in achieving organizational goals.

Team building is another area where Appreciative Inquiry and Integral Theory shine, as they focus on building strong relationships and fostering a sense of unity among team members. By emphasizing the strengths and unique contributions of each team member, leaders can create a cohesive and high-performing team that is better equipped to tackle complex challenges and achieve shared objectives. This approach not only enhances team dynamics but also promotes a culture of collaboration and mutual support within the organization.

Cultural transformation is a key component of organizational success, and Appreciative Inquiry and Integral Theory provide a comprehensive framework for driving positive change in this area. By integrating these two approaches, organizations can identify and address cultural barriers that may be hindering their growth and development. By fostering a culture of openness, trust, and collaboration, organizations can create a more inclusive and innovative work environment that is better equipped to adapt to changing market conditions and emerging trends. Ultimately, by leveraging Appreciative Inquiry and Integral Theory, corporate executives can drive positive change, foster innovation, and achieve sustainable growth in today's competitive business landscape.

The Power of Combining Appreciative Inquiry and Integral Theory

In the realm of corporate success, the combination of Appreciative Inquiry and Integral Theory has proven to be an incredibly powerful transformational framework. By blending the strengths of these two methodologies, organizations can tap into a deeper level of understanding and insight, leading to more effective and sustainable change. The synergy created by combining Appreciative Inquiry's focus on strengths and possibilities with Integral Theory's holistic and comprehensive approach allows for a more nuanced and integrated understanding of complex organizational challenges.

Leadership development is an area where Appreciative Inquiry and Integral Theory shine when combined. By using Appreciative Inquiry to identify and amplify the strengths and positive qualities of leaders, and Integral Theory to provide a comprehensive framework for leadership development, organizations can create a more robust and effective leadership pipeline. This approach not only helps to develop individual leaders but also fosters a culture of leadership excellence throughout the organization.

Organizational change is another area where the combination of Appreciative Inquiry and Integral Theory can have a profound impact. By using Appreciative Inquiry to engage stakeholders in a positive and forward-thinking dialogue about change, and Integral Theory to provide a comprehensive understanding of the various factors influencing change, organizations can navigate change more effectively and with less resistance. This approach allows organizations to harness the power of change as a positive force for growth and development.

Team building is an essential component of organizational success, and Appreciative Inquiry and Integral Theory can be powerful tools in this area as well. By using Appreciative Inquiry to uncover and amplify the strengths and talents of team members, and Integral Theory to provide a comprehensive understanding of team dynamics and interactions, organizations can build high-performing teams that are aligned and cohesive. This approach not only enhances team performance but also fosters a culture of collaboration and mutual support.

In conclusion, the power of combining Appreciative Inquiry and Integral Theory cannot be overstated. These two methodologies, when used together, create a transformational framework that can drive organizational success in a variety of areas, from leadership development to organizational change, team building to cultural transformation. By leveraging the strengths of both Appreciative Inquiry and Integral Theory, organizations can create a more resilient, effective, and sustainable future for themselves and their employees.

Benefits of Transformational Frameworks for Corporate Success

Corporate executives are constantly seeking new ways to improve their organizations and drive success. One powerful tool that has been gaining popularity in recent years is the use of transformational frameworks, specifically Appreciative Inquiry and Integral Theory. When combined, these two frameworks create a dynamic approach to corporate transformation that can lead to significant benefits for companies of all sizes.

Appreciative Inquiry and Integral Theory in Leadership Development is one area where this combination shines. By utilizing the strengths-based approach of Appreciative Inquiry and the holistic perspective of Integral Theory, executives can develop leaders who are not only effective in their roles but also capable of driving positive change within their organizations. This approach helps to create a culture of continuous learning and growth, where leaders are empowered to lead with purpose and vision.

Another key benefit of utilizing Appreciative Inquiry and Integral Theory is in organizational change. By focusing on the positive aspects of the organization and taking a comprehensive view of the systems and structures in place, executives can more effectively navigate the complexities of change management. This approach encourages collaboration and innovation, leading to a more agile and adaptive organization that can thrive in today's competitive market.

Team building is another area where Appreciative Inquiry and Integral Theory can make a significant impact. By fostering a culture of trust, collaboration, and open communication, executives can create high-performing teams that are able to achieve their goals with efficiency and effectiveness. This approach helps to break down silos and build strong relationships among team members, leading to increased productivity and employee satisfaction.

Cultural transformation is yet another area where the combination of Appreciative Inquiry and Integral Theory can be highly beneficial. By addressing the underlying beliefs, values, and assumptions that shape organizational culture, executives can create a more inclusive and diverse workplace that is better equipped to meet the challenges of today's global economy. This approach helps to foster a sense of belonging and purpose among employees, leading to higher levels of engagement and retention.

In conclusion, the benefits of utilizing Appreciative Inquiry and Integral Theory for corporate success are clear. From leadership development to organizational change, team building, cultural transformation, and beyond, this powerful combination of frameworks offers executives a comprehensive and effective approach to driving positive change within their organizations. By embracing these principles and practices, corporate executives can position their companies for long-term success in an increasingly competitive and complex business environment.

CHAPTER 2: APPRECIATIVE INQUIRY AND INTEGRAL THEORY IN LEADERSHIP DEVELOPMENT

Developing Transformational Leaders with Appreciative Inquiry and Integral Theory

In today's fast-paced and ever-changing corporate world, the need for transformational leaders has never been greater. Leaders who can inspire and motivate their teams, drive change, and create a positive organizational culture are essential for success. Developing transformational leaders requires a deep understanding of human behavior, organizational dynamics, and the principles of effective leadership. By combining Appreciative Inquiry and Integral Theory, organizations can create a powerful framework for developing transformational leaders.

Appreciative Inquiry is a strengths-based approach to organizational change that focuses on what is working well within an organization and how to build upon those strengths. Integral Theory, on the other hand, provides a comprehensive framework for understanding human development and organizational dynamics. By combining these two approaches, organizations can create a holistic and powerful framework for leadership development.

When it comes to developing transformational leaders, Appreciative Inquiry and Integral Theory offer a unique perspective on leadership development. By focusing on strengths, values, and positive organizational practices, leaders can develop a deep understanding of what motivates their teams and how to create a culture of trust and collaboration. By integrating Integral Theory, leaders can gain insights into the different stages of human development and how to effectively lead teams through change and transformation.

Utilizing Appreciative Inquiry and Integral Theory for organizational change can help leaders identify areas for improvement, build upon existing strengths, and create a shared vision for the future. By engaging employees in the change process and focusing on positive organizational practices, leaders can create a culture of innovation and continuous improvement. By integrating Integral Theory, leaders can gain insights into the different perspectives and worldviews within their organization, allowing them to create more effective change strategies.

In conclusion, developing transformational leaders with Appreciative Inquiry and Integral Theory is essential for corporate success in today's rapidly changing business environment. By combining these two powerful frameworks, organizations can create a culture of trust, collaboration, and innovation. By focusing on strengths, values, and positive organizational practices, leaders can inspire their teams to achieve their full potential and drive organizational success.

Building Leadership Capacity through Positive Inquiry

Building leadership capacity is essential for long-term success. One of the most powerful tools for developing leadership skills is through the practice of positive inquiry. By focusing on strengths, possibilities, and what is working well within an organization, leaders can inspire and motivate their teams to achieve greatness.

Appreciative Inquiry and Integral Theory have been combined to create a transformational framework that can help corporate executives unlock their full potential as leaders. By utilizing the principles of Appreciative Inquiry, which focus on positive change and growth, and Integral Theory, which emphasizes a holistic approach to leadership development, executives can create a culture of continuous learning and improvement within their organizations.

By applying Appreciative Inquiry and Integral Theory to leadership development, executives can foster a culture of collaboration, innovation, and empowerment within their teams. By focusing on what is going well and building on strengths, leaders can inspire their teams to achieve greatness and drive organizational success.

When it comes to team building, Appreciative Inquiry and Integral Theory can help executives create high-performing teams that are aligned with the organization's goals and values. By leveraging the principles of Appreciative Inquiry, which focus on building positive relationships and fostering a culture of trust and respect, leaders can create teams that are motivated, engaged, and committed to achieving shared goals.

Ultimately, by integrating Appreciative Inquiry and Integral Theory into their leadership development efforts, corporate executives can create a culture of continuous improvement, innovation, and success within their organizations. By focusing on strengths, possibilities, and what is working well, leaders can inspire and motivate their teams to achieve greatness and drive organizational success.

Integrating Integral Theory into Leadership Development Programs

In the world of corporate leadership development, there is

a growing recognition of the power of integrating Integral Theory into existing programs. Integral Theory, developed by philosopher Ken Wilber, offers a comprehensive framework for understanding and addressing the complexity of human behavior and organizational dynamics. When combined with Appreciative Inquiry, a strengths-based approach to organizational change, the result is a powerful transformational framework that can drive corporate success.

Leadership development programs that incorporate both Appreciative Inquiry and Integral Theory are able to tap into the full potential of individuals and teams within an organization. By focusing on strengths and possibilities, rather than weaknesses and problems, leaders can inspire and empower their teams to achieve greater levels of performance and innovation. This approach fosters a culture of positivity and collaboration, leading to enhanced employee engagement and organizational success.

Utilizing Appreciative Inquiry and Integral Theory for organizational change allows leaders to create a shared vision and purpose that aligns with the values and goals of the organization. By engaging stakeholders in a process of discovery and co-creation, leaders can build consensus and commitment around a common direction. This approach not only facilitates change initiatives, but also builds resilience and adaptability within the organization to navigate future challenges.

Applying Appreciative Inquiry and Integral Theory for team building is essential for creating high-performing teams that are able to collaborate effectively and achieve results. By understanding the individual strengths and perspectives of team members within the context of the larger organizational system, leaders can foster a sense of unity and cohesion. This approach promotes trust, communication, and accountability, leading to improved team dynamics and outcomes.

Integrating Appreciative Inquiry and Integral Theory for cultural transformation is key to creating a workplace environment that values diversity, inclusion, and authenticity. By exploring the multiple dimensions of culture – including beliefs, values, behaviors, and systems – leaders can identify opportunities for growth and change. This approach allows organizations to embrace complexity and ambiguity, leading to a culture of continuous learning and innovation. By leveraging the power of Appreciative Inquiry and Integral Theory, corporate executives can create a lasting impact on their organizations and drive sustainable success in today's rapidly changing business landscape.

CHAPTER 3: UTILIZING APPRECIATIVE INQUIRY AND INTEGRAL THEORY FOR ORGANIZATIONAL CHANGE

Creating Sustainable Change through Appreciative Inquiry

Creating sustainable change through Appreciative Inquiry is a powerful approach that can revolutionize the way corporations operate. By combining Appreciative Inquiry and Integral Theory, corporate executives can tap into the most effective transformational framework available. This innovative approach not only focuses on problem-solving but also on leveraging strengths and positive aspects within the organization to create lasting change.

Leadership development is a key area where Appreciative Inquiry and Integral Theory can make a significant impact. By utilizing these frameworks, executives can identify and amplify the strengths of their team members, leading to increased engagement, motivation, and overall performance. This approach fosters a culture of empowerment and growth, where employees feel valued and supported in their professional development.

Organizational change is another area where Appreciative Inquiry and Integral Theory shine. By focusing on the positive aspects of the organization and building on its strengths, leaders can create a more adaptive and resilient workplace. This approach encourages a shift in mindset from problem-focused to possibility-focused, leading to more successful and sustainable change initiatives.

Team building is essential for a cohesive and high-performing workforce. By applying Appreciative Inquiry and Integral Theory, corporate executives can create teams that are not only effective but also collaborative and innovative. This approach encourages team members to appreciate each other's strengths and contributions, leading to a more harmonious and productive work environment.

Cultural transformation is a daunting task for many organizations, but with the integration of Appreciative Inquiry and Integral Theory, it becomes more manageable. By focusing on the positive aspects of the organization's culture and aligning it with the organization's values and goals, leaders can create a more inclusive and vibrant culture. This approach fosters a sense of belonging and purpose among employees, leading to increased employee engagement and satisfaction.

In conclusion, Appreciative Inquiry and Integral Theory offer a powerful and holistic approach to corporate success. By incorporating these frameworks into leadership development, organizational change, team building, cultural transformation, and other key areas, corporate executives can create sustainable change that leads to enhanced performance, innovation, and employee engagement. It is time for corporations to embrace these transformational frameworks and unlock their full potential for success.

Aligning Values and Beliefs with Integral Theory

Aligning values and beliefs with Integral Theory is essential for corporate executives looking to create a cohesive and successful organization. By understanding and integrating Integral Theory into their leadership practices, executives can align their values and beliefs with a holistic approach to problem-solving and decision-making. This alignment allows for a deeper understanding of the interconnectedness of all aspects of the organization, from individual team members to the overall corporate culture.

Appreciative Inquiry and Integral Theory combined create a powerful transformational framework for corporations, as they focus on strengths, possibilities, and interconnectedness. By utilizing Appreciative Inquiry to identify and amplify what is working well within the organization, and integrating Integral Theory to understand the complexity and interconnectedness of all aspects of the organization, executives can create a more resilient and sustainable business model. This approach not only fosters a positive work environment but also leads to long-term success and growth.

In leadership development, Appreciative Inquiry and Integral Theory provide a comprehensive framework for executives to cultivate a strong sense of self-awareness and align their values and beliefs with their leadership practices. By understanding how their personal values and beliefs impact their decision-making processes, executives can lead with integrity and authenticity. This alignment creates a solid foundation for building trust and fostering a positive organizational culture.

When it comes to organizational change, utilizing Appreciative Inquiry and Integral Theory can help executives navigate through transitions more effectively. By focusing on strengths and possibilities, rather than problems and deficits, executives can create a more positive and empowering approach to change management. Integrating Integral Theory allows executives to understand the complexity of organizational systems and make informed decisions that align with the organization's values and beliefs.

In conclusion, aligning values and beliefs with Integral Theory is crucial for corporate executives looking to create a successful and sustainable organization. By integrating Appreciative Inquiry and Integral Theory into their leadership practices, executives can foster a positive work environment, lead with integrity and authenticity, navigate through organizational change more effectively, and ultimately drive long-term success and growth. This powerful transformational framework provides a holistic approach to problem-solving, decision-making, and organizational development, leading to a more resilient and sustainable business model.

Overcoming Resistance to Change with Positive Inquiry

In the corporate world, change is inevitable. However, resistance to change can often hinder progress and innovation within an organization. As corporate executives, it is essential to find effective strategies to overcome this resistance and foster a culture of positive transformation. One powerful approach to managing change is through the use of Appreciative Inquiry and Integral Theory.

Appreciative Inquiry is a strengths-based approach to organizational development that focuses on identifying and building upon what is working well within an organization. Integral Theory, on the other hand, provides a comprehensive framework for understanding and addressing the complexities of organizational change. When these two methodologies are combined, they create a powerful transformational framework that can help corporate executives navigate through resistance to change.

One key strategy for overcoming resistance to change with Positive Inquiry is to focus on the positive aspects of the change rather than dwelling on the negatives. By asking questions that highlight what is working well and what can be improved upon, executives can create a sense of excitement and possibility around the change process. This approach helps to shift the focus from fear and resistance to optimism and engagement.

Another important aspect of utilizing Appreciative Inquiry and Integral Theory for organizational change is to involve employees at all levels of the organization in the change process. By soliciting input and feedback from employees, executives can gain valuable insights into potential barriers to change and develop strategies to address them effectively. This participatory approach not only fosters a sense of ownership and commitment among employees but also helps to build a culture of collaboration and innovation within the organization.

In conclusion, overcoming resistance to change with Positive Inquiry is a powerful tool for corporate executives seeking to drive transformation and achieve success within their organizations. By leveraging the principles of Appreciative Inquiry and Integral Theory, executives can create a culture of positivity, collaboration, and innovation that will enable their organizations to thrive in today's rapidly changing business environment. By embracing change and approaching it with curiosity and optimism, corporate executives can lead their organizations to new heights of success and growth.

CHAPTER 4: APPLYING APPRECIATIVE INQUIRY AND INTEGRAL THEORY FOR TEAM BUILDING

Fostering Collaboration and Trust within Teams

Fostering collaboration and trust within teams is crucial for the success of any organization. In today's fast-paced and ever-changing business environment, it is more important than ever for corporate executives to understand the power of working together and building strong relationships within their teams. By utilizing a combination of Appreciative Inquiry and Integral Theory, executives can create a framework that promotes collaboration and trust among team members.

Appreciative Inquiry is a powerful approach that focuses on building on the strengths and successes of individuals and teams, rather than focusing on problems and weaknesses. By using this approach in conjunction with Integral Theory, which emphasizes the importance of considering all aspects of a situation in order to create holistic solutions, executives can create a transformative framework for fostering collaboration and trust within their teams.

Leadership development is another key area where Appreciative

Inquiry and Integral Theory can be utilized to create a positive impact. By focusing on strengths and successes, leaders can inspire and motivate their teams to work together towards a common goal. By incorporating Integral Theory into leadership development, executives can ensure that they are considering all aspects of their leadership style and how it impacts their team's ability to collaborate and trust one another.

Organizational change is inevitable in today's business world, and it is important for executives to be able to navigate these changes effectively. By utilizing Appreciative Inquiry and Integral Theory, executives can create a framework for managing change that promotes collaboration and trust within their teams. By focusing on strengths and successes, executives can inspire their teams to embrace change and work together towards a common goal.

In conclusion, by incorporating Appreciative Inquiry and Integral Theory into team building, leadership development, organizational change, and other areas of corporate success, executives can create a powerful framework for fostering collaboration and trust within their teams. By focusing on strengths and successes, considering all aspects of a situation, and inspiring their teams to work together towards a common goal, executives can create a culture of collaboration and trust that will drive their organization towards success.

Enhancing Team Dynamics through Appreciative Inquiry

In the fast-paced and ever-changing world of corporate business, team dynamics play a crucial role in the success of an organization. One powerful tool that corporate executives can use to enhance team dynamics is Appreciative Inquiry. Appreciative Inquiry is a strength-based approach to organizational development that focuses on what is working well within a team or organization, rather than on what is not working. By using Appreciative Inquiry, corporate executives can foster a positive and collaborative team environment that encourages creativity, innovation, and high performance.

When combined with Integral Theory, Appreciative Inquiry becomes even more powerful in enhancing team dynamics. Integral Theory provides a comprehensive framework for understanding and addressing the complex and interconnected nature of organizations. By integrating Appreciative Inquiry and Integral Theory, corporate executives can gain a deeper understanding of their team dynamics and develop strategies to improve communication, collaboration, and overall team effectiveness.

Leadership development is another area where Appreciative Inquiry and Integral Theory can be utilized to enhance team dynamics. By focusing on the strengths and positive qualities of team members, leaders can inspire and motivate their teams to achieve greater success. Appreciative Inquiry and Integral Theory provide leaders with the tools and strategies to create a supportive and empowering environment that fosters growth and development among team members.

Organizational change is inevitable in today's business world, and corporate executives can utilize Appreciative Inquiry and Integral Theory to navigate through periods of transition and transformation. By focusing on what is working well within the organization and building on its strengths, leaders can guide their teams through change with confidence and resilience. Appreciative Inquiry and Integral Theory help organizations adapt to new challenges and opportunities, while maintaining a strong sense of purpose and unity among team members.

In conclusion, Appreciative Inquiry and Integral Theory offer a powerful framework for enhancing team dynamics in corporate organizations. By focusing on strengths, positive qualities, and interconnectedness, corporate executives can create a collaborative and high-performing team environment that drives success and innovation. Whether used for leadership development, organizational change, team building, or cultural transformation, Appreciative Inquiry and Integral Theory provide corporate executives with the tools and strategies they need to maximize performance, foster employee engagement, and create a positive and productive work culture.

Using Integral Theory to Improve Team Performance

In today's fast-paced corporate world, team performance is essential for success. As corporate executives, it is crucial to constantly seek out new and innovative ways to improve team dynamics and drive performance. One powerful approach that has been gaining traction in recent years is the use of Integral Theory to enhance team effectiveness. Integral Theory, developed by philosopher Ken Wilber, offers a comprehensive framework for understanding human behavior and organizational dynamics. By incorporating Integral Theory into team development strategies, executives can gain valuable insights into the complex interplay of individual personalities, group dynamics, and organizational culture.

Applying Integral Theory to team performance involves taking a holistic approach that considers multiple perspectives and dimensions of human experience. This means looking beyond traditional models of team building and leadership development to explore the deeper, more nuanced aspects of human behavior and interaction. By incorporating Integral Theory into team development initiatives, executives can gain a deeper understanding of the unique strengths and weaknesses of their teams, as well as the underlying factors that may be influencing performance. This broader perspective can help executives identify areas for improvement and develop more effective strategies for enhancing team performance.

One key benefit of using Integral Theory to improve team performance is its emphasis on diversity and inclusivity. Integral Theory recognizes that individuals bring a wide range of perspectives, skills, and experiences to the table, and that harnessing this diversity can lead to more innovative and effective team dynamics. By incorporating Integral Theory into team development initiatives, executives can create a culture of inclusivity that values and leverages the unique contributions of each team member. This can lead to greater creativity, collaboration, and overall team performance.

Another important aspect of using Integral Theory to improve team performance is its focus on personal and collective growth. Integral Theory posits that individuals and groups evolve through multiple stages of development, each with its own unique challenges and opportunities. By incorporating Integral Theory into team development strategies, executives can help team members identify their current stage of development and work towards higher levels of growth and self-awareness. This can lead to greater personal fulfillment, stronger team cohesion, and ultimately, improved team performance.

In conclusion, incorporating Integral Theory into team development initiatives can be a powerful tool for enhancing team performance in today's corporate environment. By taking a holistic approach that considers multiple perspectives and dimensions of human experience, executives can gain valuable insights into the complex dynamics of their teams and develop more effective strategies for driving performance. By embracing diversity, fostering inclusivity, and promoting personal and collective growth, executives can create a culture of excellence that empowers teams to reach their full potential. Ultimately, by utilizing Integral Theory to improve team performance, executives can create a more engaged, collaborative, and high-performing workforce that is poised for success in the rapidly evolving business landscape.

CHAPTER 5: INTEGRATING APPRECIATIVE INQUIRY AND INTEGRAL THEORY FOR CULTURAL TRANSFORMATION

Shifting Organizational Culture with Positive Inquiry

In today's rapidly changing business environment, corporate executives are constantly seeking new ways to transform their organizations and drive success. One powerful approach that has gained traction in recent years is the combination of Appreciative Inquiry and Integral Theory. By integrating these two frameworks, executives can create a holistic approach to organizational transformation that addresses both individual and collective needs.

Appreciative Inquiry and Integral Theory in Leadership Development

Leadership development is a key priority for many organizations looking to drive growth and innovation. By incorporating

Appreciative Inquiry and Integral Theory into leadership development programs, executives can help their leaders tap into their full potential and lead with purpose and passion. This approach not only enhances individual leadership skills but also fosters a culture of collaboration and empowerment within the organization.

Utilizing Appreciative Inquiry and Integral Theory for Organizational Change

Organizational change can be a daunting process, but by leveraging the power of Appreciative Inquiry and Integral Theory, executives can navigate change more effectively. These frameworks provide a structured approach to change management that focuses on building on strengths and creating a shared vision for the future. By engaging employees in the change process and fostering a culture of positivity and collaboration, organizations can achieve lasting transformation.

Applying Appreciative Inquiry and Integral Theory for Team Building

Effective teamwork is essential for driving success in today's complex business landscape. By incorporating Appreciative Inquiry and Integral Theory into team-building initiatives, executives can create high-performing teams that are aligned around a shared vision and purpose. This approach helps teams leverage their collective strengths and work together towards common goals, leading to increased productivity and innovation.

Integrating Appreciative Inquiry and Integral Theory for Cultural Transformation

Organizational culture plays a crucial role in shaping employee behavior and driving business outcomes. By integrating Appreciative Inquiry and Integral Theory into cultural transformation initiatives, executives can create a culture that is aligned with the organization's values and goals. This approach helps organizations foster a positive work environment where employees feel engaged, motivated, and empowered to contribute their best work.

Creating a Culture of Innovation with Integral Theory

Creating a culture of innovation within a corporate setting can be a challenging task, but with the integration of Appreciative Inquiry and Integral Theory, it becomes not only achievable but also sustainable. By combining these two powerful frameworks, corporate executives can tap into the full potential of their organization and drive real transformational change.

Appreciative Inquiry focuses on the strengths and positive aspects of an organization, while Integral Theory provides a comprehensive and holistic approach to understanding and addressing complex issues. When used together, these frameworks can help leaders identify opportunities for growth, foster creativity and collaboration, and ultimately drive innovation throughout the organization.

In leadership development, Appreciative Inquiry and Integral Theory can be used to cultivate a culture of continuous learning and growth. By focusing on strengths and leveraging the integral framework to address multiple dimensions of leadership, executives can develop the skills and mindset needed to lead with innovation and adaptability.

For organizational change, the combination of Appreciative Inquiry and Integral Theory offers a powerful approach to navigating and managing transitions. By engaging employees in the change process, leveraging strengths, and addressing all aspects of the organization, leaders can create a positive and sustainable transformation that drives innovation and growth.

Team building is another area where Appreciative Inquiry and Integral Theory can make a significant impact. By fostering a culture of collaboration, communication, and mutual respect, leaders can create high-performing teams that are primed for innovation and success. By utilizing the strengths-based approach of Appreciative Inquiry and the comprehensive perspective of Integral Theory, teams can work together more effectively and produce innovative solutions to complex challenges.

Promoting Diversity and Inclusion through Appreciative Inquiry

In today's rapidly changing business landscape, promoting diversity and inclusion has become a top priority for many organizations. By embracing diversity and fostering an inclusive work environment, companies can tap into a wealth of perspectives and experiences that can drive innovation and creativity. One powerful tool that corporate executives can use to promote diversity and inclusion is Appreciative Inquiry.

Appreciative Inquiry is a strengths-based approach to organizational development that focuses on what is working well within an organization, rather than on its problems or deficiencies. By using Appreciative Inquiry, corporate executives can create a culture that values diversity and inclusion, and celebrates the unique contributions of every individual within the organization. This approach can help to break down barriers and foster a sense of belonging among employees from diverse backgrounds.

When combined with Integral Theory, Appreciative Inquiry becomes an even more powerful tool for promoting diversity and inclusion within organizations. Integral Theory provides a comprehensive framework for understanding and addressing the complex challenges that organizations face, including those related to diversity and inclusion. By integrating Appreciative Inquiry and Integral Theory, corporate executives can develop a holistic approach to promoting diversity and inclusion that takes into account the multiple dimensions of diversity, such as race, gender, age, and cultural background.

One way that corporate executives can utilize Appreciative

Inquiry and Integral Theory to promote diversity and inclusion is through leadership development. By incorporating these frameworks into leadership training programs, executives can equip leaders with the skills and knowledge they need to effectively promote diversity and inclusion within their teams. This can help to create a more inclusive and welcoming work environment, where all employees feel valued and respected.

In addition to leadership development, corporate executives can also apply Appreciative Inquiry and Integral Theory to organizational change initiatives. By using these frameworks to guide change efforts, executives can ensure that diversity and inclusion are prioritized throughout the organization. This can help to create a more diverse and inclusive workplace culture, where all employees have the opportunity to thrive and succeed. By leveraging the power of Appreciative Inquiry and Integral Theory, corporate executives can promote diversity and inclusion within their organizations, driving innovation, creativity, and success.

CHAPTER 6: USING APPRECIATIVE INQUIRY AND INTEGRAL THEORY FOR EMPLOYEE ENGAGEMENT

Increasing Employee Motivation and Satisfaction

In today's competitive business landscape, it is crucial for corporate executives to focus on increasing employee motivation and satisfaction in order to drive success and achieve sustainable growth. By utilizing the powerful combination of Appreciative Inquiry and Integral Theory, companies can create a transformational framework that fosters a positive work environment and empowers employees to reach their full potential.

Appreciative Inquiry is a strength-based approach that focuses on identifying and building upon the positive aspects of an organization, while Integral Theory provides a comprehensive framework for understanding and addressing the complex dynamics of corporate culture. When these two methodologies are integrated, corporate executives have a powerful tool at their disposal for driving organizational change and promoting employee engagement.

One key aspect of increasing employee motivation and satisfaction is leadership development. By utilizing Appreciative Inquiry and Integral Theory in leadership development programs, executives can empower their managers to lead with vision, purpose, and authenticity. This approach not only enhances individual leadership skills, but also fosters a culture of trust, collaboration, and innovation throughout the organization.

Another important application of Appreciative Inquiry and Integral Theory is in team building. By leveraging the strengths of team members and fostering a culture of appreciation and inclusivity, executives can create high-performing teams that are motivated, engaged, and aligned towards achieving common goals. This approach not only enhances team dynamics, but also improves communication, collaboration, and overall team effectiveness.

Furthermore, by integrating Appreciative Inquiry and Integral Theory into strategic planning processes, corporate executives can align organizational goals with employee values and aspirations, leading to greater employee engagement and buy-in. This approach enables companies to create strategic plans that are not only innovative and forward-thinking, but also grounded in the collective wisdom and insights of employees at all levels of the organization. Ultimately, by prioritizing employee motivation and satisfaction through the lens of Appreciative Inquiry and Integral Theory, corporate executives can create a culture of excellence, empowerment, and continuous improvement that drives long-term success and sustainable growth.

Empowering Employees through Positive Inquiry

In the world of corporate leadership, empowering employees is crucial for creating a positive and productive work environment. One powerful method for achieving this is through the practice of positive inquiry. Positive inquiry is a process that focuses on the strengths and potential of individuals, rather than their weaknesses or limitations. By utilizing positive inquiry, corporate executives can inspire and motivate their employees to reach their full potential.

When positive inquiry is combined with integral theory, the result is a transformational framework that can revolutionize the way corporations operate. Integral theory provides a comprehensive approach to understanding and addressing the complexities of organizational dynamics. By integrating integral theory into their leadership development strategies, corporate executives can gain a deeper understanding of their employees' needs and motivations, leading to more effective and sustainable outcomes.

One of the key benefits of incorporating positive inquiry and integral theory into leadership development is the ability to foster a culture of continuous growth and improvement within the organization. By utilizing positive inquiry techniques, corporate executives can help their employees identify and leverage their strengths, leading to increased engagement, satisfaction, and productivity. When combined with integral theory, this approach can create a powerful framework for organizational change that is both sustainable and transformative.

Team building is another area where positive inquiry and integral theory can have a significant impact. By using positive inquiry techniques to identify and build upon the strengths of individual team members, corporate executives can create cohesive and high-performing teams. When integrated with integral theory, this approach can help teams navigate complex challenges and achieve their goals more effectively.

In conclusion, the combination of appreciative inquiry and integral theory offers corporate executives a powerful framework for empowering employees and driving organizational success. By utilizing these approaches in leadership development, organizational change, team building, and cultural transformation, executives can create a work environment that is conducive to innovation, collaboration, and high performance. By incorporating positive inquiry and integral theory into their strategic planning, communication, conflict resolution, and performance management processes, corporate leaders can unlock the full potential of their employees and achieve sustainable success.

Building a Culture of Appreciation and Recognition

Building a culture of appreciation and recognition is essential for the success of any corporation. By implementing the principles of Appreciative Inquiry and Integral Theory, corporate executives can create a work environment that fosters positivity, collaboration, and innovation. Appreciative Inquiry is a powerful tool for shifting organizational culture towards a more positive and strengths-based approach. By focusing on what is working well within the organization and amplifying those successes, executives can inspire a culture of appreciation and recognition.

Integral Theory provides a comprehensive framework for understanding and addressing the complexities of organizational dynamics. By integrating Appreciative Inquiry and Integral Theory, corporate executives can develop a holistic approach to building a culture of appreciation and recognition. This approach takes into account the interconnected nature of various organizational elements, such as leadership, communication, and employee engagement. By aligning these elements with a common vision of appreciation and recognition, executives can create a unified and cohesive culture within their organization.

Leadership development is a key aspect of building a culture of appreciation and recognition. By utilizing Appreciative Inquiry and Integral Theory in leadership development programs, executives can empower their leaders to become catalysts for positive change within the organization. Leaders who embody the principles of appreciation and recognition can inspire their teams to excel and achieve greater levels of success. By integrating

Appreciative Inquiry and Integral Theory into leadership development initiatives, executives can cultivate a culture of appreciation and recognition from the top down.

Organizational change is inevitable in today's fast-paced business environment. By utilizing Appreciative Inquiry and Integral Theory for organizational change, corporate executives can navigate change more effectively and sustainably. These frameworks provide a roadmap for engaging employees in the change process, fostering a sense of appreciation and recognition for their contributions. By incorporating Appreciative Inquiry and Integral Theory into their change management strategies, executives can ensure that their organization emerges stronger and more resilient in the face of change.

In conclusion, building a culture of appreciation and recognition is vital for the long-term success of any corporation. By integrating Appreciative Inquiry and Integral Theory into their organizational practices, corporate executives can create a work environment that values and celebrates the contributions of all employees. This approach not only improves employee engagement and morale but also enhances overall performance and innovation within the organization. By embracing the principles of Appreciative Inquiry and Integral Theory, corporate executives can transform their organization into a place where appreciation and recognition are at the core of its culture.

CHAPTER 7: INCORPORATING APPRECIATIVE INQUIRY AND INTEGRAL THEORY IN STRATEGIC PLANNING

Aligning Vision and Mission with Integral Theory

In the world of corporate success, aligning vision and mission with Integral Theory is crucial for sustainable growth and transformation. Integral Theory provides a comprehensive framework that encompasses all aspects of an organization, from individual development to cultural transformation. By integrating Integral Theory with Appreciative Inquiry, corporate executives can create a powerful transformational framework that fosters positive change and innovation.

Appreciative Inquiry is a strengths-based approach that focuses on what is working well within an organization, rather than solely on its problems. When combined with Integral Theory, this approach can help leaders identify and leverage the unique strengths and capabilities of their teams, leading to increased engagement and productivity. By aligning the vision and mission of the organization with Integral Theory principles, executives can create a roadmap for success that is grounded in a deep understanding of the interconnectedness of all aspects of the organization.

Leadership development is another area where Appreciative Inquiry and Integral Theory can have a profound impact. By utilizing these frameworks, executives can foster a culture of continuous learning and growth within their organizations. By aligning their leadership development initiatives with Integral Theory principles, executives can ensure that their leaders are equipped with the knowledge and skills needed to navigate the complex challenges of today's business environment.

Organizational change is a constant in today's fast-paced world, and utilizing Appreciative Inquiry and Integral Theory can help executives navigate these changes with grace and agility. By applying these frameworks to change management initiatives, executives can ensure that their organizations are able to adapt and thrive in the face of uncertainty. By aligning their change management efforts with Integral Theory principles, executives can create a culture of resilience and innovation that will propel their organizations to new heights of success.

In conclusion, aligning vision and mission with Integral Theory is essential for corporate executives looking to create sustainable growth and transformation within their organizations. By integrating Appreciative Inquiry and Integral Theory, executives can create a powerful transformational framework that fosters positive change and innovation. Whether it's leadership development, organizational change, team building, or cultural transformation, Appreciative Inquiry and Integral Theory provide executives with the tools they need to succeed in today's dynamic business environment.

Developing Strategic Plans with Positive Inquiry

Developing strategic plans with positive inquiry is a crucial aspect of corporate success in today's competitive business environment. By combining the principles of Appreciative Inquiry and Integral Theory, corporate executives can create a powerful transformational framework that drives organizational growth and innovation. Appreciative Inquiry focuses on identifying and amplifying the positive aspects of an organization, while Integral Theory provides a comprehensive approach to understanding the complexities of systems and structures within a corporation.

In leadership development, utilizing Appreciative Inquiry and Integral Theory can help executives identify their strengths and leverage them to inspire and motivate their teams. By focusing on what is working well within the organization, leaders can create a culture of positivity and collaboration that drives performance and results. This approach can also help leaders identify areas for growth and development, leading to more effective leadership practices and strategies.

When it comes to organizational change, Appreciative Inquiry and Integral Theory provide a structured framework for guiding the transformation process. By focusing on the positive aspects of the organization and aligning them with the strategic goals and objectives, executives can create a roadmap for change that is both effective and sustainable. This approach can help organizations adapt to changing market conditions, technology advancements, and customer demands, ensuring long-term success and viability.

Team building is another area where Appreciative Inquiry and Integral Theory can be highly effective. By leveraging the strengths and talents of team members, executives can create high-performing teams that are aligned with the organization's mission and vision. This approach fosters collaboration, creativity, and innovation, leading to increased productivity and engagement among team members. By focusing on what is working well within the team, leaders can build trust and rapport, leading to stronger relationships and better communication.

In conclusion, integrating Appreciative Inquiry and Integral Theory into strategic planning is essential for driving organizational growth and success. By focusing on the positive aspects of the organization, leaders can create a culture of positivity and collaboration that drives performance and results. This approach can help organizations adapt to change, build high-performing teams, and drive innovation and creativity. By leveraging the power of Appreciative Inquiry and Integral Theory, corporate executives can create a transformational framework that leads to long-term success and sustainability.

Achieving Strategic Goals through Appreciative Inquiry

Achieving strategic goals through Appreciative Inquiry is a powerful tool that can help corporate executives navigate the complexities of today's business world. By combining Appreciative Inquiry with Integral Theory, organizations can create a transformational framework that drives success and growth. This subchapter will explore how these two methodologies can be integrated to achieve strategic goals and drive organizational success.

Leadership development is a critical aspect of any organization's success. By utilizing Appreciative Inquiry and Integral Theory, corporate executives can create a leadership development program that fosters growth and innovation. These methodologies focus on strengths and possibilities, rather than weaknesses and problems, ensuring that leaders are equipped to navigate challenges and inspire their teams to achieve greatness.

Organizational change is inevitable in today's fast-paced business environment. By applying Appreciative Inquiry and Integral Theory, corporate executives can effectively manage change and drive transformation within their organizations. These methodologies focus on engaging employees in the change process, ensuring that everyone is aligned towards a common goal and working together to achieve success.

Team building is essential for creating a strong and cohesive workforce. By integrating Appreciative Inquiry and Integral Theory, corporate executives can build high-performing teams that are capable of achieving extraordinary results. These methodologies focus on building trust, fostering collaboration, and celebrating success, creating a positive and productive team dynamic.

Cultural transformation is key to creating a thriving and successful organization. By using Appreciative Inquiry and Integral Theory, corporate executives can create a culture of positivity, collaboration, and innovation. These methodologies focus on engaging employees in the transformation process, ensuring that everyone feels valued and empowered to contribute to the organization's success. By leveraging Appreciative Inquiry and Integral Theory, corporate executives can create a culture that fosters employee engagement, drives innovation, enhances communication, resolves conflicts, maximizes performance, and ultimately achieves strategic goals.

CHAPTER 8: ENHANCING COMMUNICATION WITH APPRECIATIVE INQUIRY AND INTEGRAL THEORY

Improving Communication Channels within Organizations

Effective communication is the cornerstone of any successful organization. In today's fast-paced business world, it is more important than ever for corporate executives to focus on improving communication channels within their organizations. By utilizing the power of Appreciative Inquiry and Integral Theory, corporate leaders can create a transformational framework that fosters open, honest, and productive communication among team members at all levels.

Appreciative Inquiry and Integral Theory combined to make the most powerful transformational framework for corporations. By integrating these two powerful methodologies, corporate executives can tap into the strengths and potential of their teams, leading to increased collaboration, innovation, and overall success. This unique approach to organizational development emphasizes the importance of positive communication and mutual respect, creating a culture of trust and transparency within the organization.

Utilizing Appreciative Inquiry and Integral Theory for organizational change is essential for driving meaningful and lasting transformation. By engaging employees in the change process and encouraging open dialogue, corporate leaders can ensure that everyone is on board with the new direction. This approach not only improves communication channels but also fosters a sense of ownership and commitment among team members, leading to greater buy-in and successful implementation of organizational changes.

Applying Appreciative Inquiry and Integral Theory for team building can help corporate executives create high-performing teams that are cohesive, collaborative, and results-driven. By leveraging the strengths and talents of individual team members, leaders can build a culture of teamwork and communication that fuels creativity and productivity. This approach not only improves communication channels within teams but also enhances overall team performance and effectiveness.

Integrating Appreciative Inquiry and Integral Theory for cultural transformation is key to creating a positive and inclusive organizational culture. By fostering a culture of appreciation, respect, and understanding, corporate leaders can break down communication barriers and create a more harmonious work environment. This approach not only improves communication channels within the organization but also enhances employee engagement, morale, and overall satisfaction. By leveraging the power of Appreciative Inquiry and Integral Theory, corporate executives can create a culture of open communication, collaboration, and innovation that drives organizational success.

Building Trust and Transparency through Positive Inquiry

In the fast-paced and ever-evolving world of corporate leadership, trust and transparency are essential foundations for success. As corporate executives, it is crucial to cultivate these qualities within your organization in order to foster a culture of collaboration, innovation, and high performance. One powerful tool for building trust and transparency is through the practice of Positive Inquiry, a core principle of Appreciative Inquiry and Integral Theory.

Positive Inquiry is a method of questioning and dialogue that focuses on the strengths, successes, and positive experiences within an organization. By shifting the focus from problems and deficits to possibilities and opportunities, Positive Inquiry creates a space for open and honest communication, mutual understanding, and shared goals. This approach not only builds trust among team members, but also encourages transparency and accountability at all levels of the organization.

By incorporating Positive Inquiry into your leadership development strategies, you can empower your team members to engage in meaningful conversations, share their unique perspectives, and contribute their talents and skills towards common objectives. This not only enhances individual growth and development, but also strengthens the bonds of trust and collaboration within the organization.

Utilizing Appreciative Inquiry and Integral Theory for organizational change can be a transformative process that aligns the values, beliefs, and behaviors of all stakeholders towards a shared vision of success. By focusing on what is working well within the organization and leveraging those strengths to drive change, leaders can inspire confidence, motivation, and commitment among team members. This approach encourages transparency by creating a culture of openness, feedback, and continuous improvement.

Applying Appreciative Inquiry and Integral Theory for team building can help create a cohesive and high-performing team that is united by a common purpose, shared values, and mutual respect. By fostering a culture of trust, transparency, and positive communication, leaders can empower team members to collaborate effectively, solve complex problems, and achieve their collective goals. This not only enhances team dynamics and productivity, but also builds a strong foundation for long-term success.

In conclusion, by integrating Appreciative Inquiry and Integral Theory into your organizational culture, you can create a workplace environment that is built on trust, transparency, and positive inquiry. By leveraging the power of these transformational frameworks, corporate executives can inspire innovation, drive performance, and enhance communication within their organizations. By incorporating these principles into your leadership development, team building, and organizational change strategies, you can foster a culture of collaboration, engagement, and success that will drive your organization towards its full potential.

Enhancing Listening Skills with Integral Theory

Listening is a crucial skill in any corporate setting, as it fosters understanding, collaboration, and innovation. By incorporating Integral Theory into your approach to listening, you can enhance your ability to truly hear and comprehend the perspectives of others. Integral Theory provides a comprehensive framework that takes into account multiple dimensions of human experience, including cognitive, emotional, and somatic aspects. By understanding these dimensions, you can become a more empathetic and attentive listener, leading to more effective communication and problem-solving within your organization.

Incorporating Integral Theory into your listening practices can also help you to better navigate the complexities of corporate dynamics. By recognizing and integrating different perspectives, values, and worldviews, you can create a more inclusive and supportive environment for your team members. This inclusive approach to listening can help to build trust, foster creativity, and drive performance within your organization. By engaging with others in a more holistic and integrated way, you can unlock new possibilities for growth and success.

Applying Integral Theory to your listening skills can also help you to become a more effective leader. By understanding the different developmental stages of individuals within your team, you can tailor your communication and feedback to meet their specific needs. This personalized approach to leadership can help to motivate and inspire your team members, leading to increased engagement and productivity. By actively listening to the concerns and aspirations of your team, you can create a more supportive and empowering work environment, where everyone feels valued and heard.

Utilizing Integral Theory to enhance your listening skills can also be instrumental in driving organizational change. By engaging with stakeholders at all levels of the organization, you can gain a deeper understanding of the challenges and opportunities facing your company. This comprehensive approach to listening can help you to identify key areas for improvement and develop innovative strategies for transformation. By incorporating diverse perspectives and insights into your decision-making processes, you can create a more adaptive and responsive organization, capable of thriving in an ever-changing business landscape.

In conclusion, by integrating Integral Theory into your approach to listening, you can unlock new possibilities for growth, collaboration, and success within your organization. By recognizing and valuing the diverse perspectives and experiences of your team members, you can create a more inclusive and dynamic work environment. By applying this holistic and integrated approach to listening, you can become a more effective leader, driving organizational change and innovation. Ultimately, by enhancing your listening skills with Integral Theory, you can cultivate a culture of openness, empathy, and creativity, leading to increased performance and success for your company.

CHAPTER 9: IMPLEMENTING APPRECIATIVE INQUIRY AND INTEGRAL THEORY FOR INNOVATION

Fostering a Culture of Creativity and Innovation

Fostering a culture of creativity and innovation is essential for corporations looking to stay competitive in today's rapidly changing business landscape. By combining the principles of Appreciative Inquiry and Integral Theory, companies can create a powerful transformational framework that encourages creativity, fosters innovation, and drives success.

Appreciative Inquiry and Integral Theory in Leadership Development go hand in hand when it comes to fostering a culture of creativity and innovation. Leaders who embrace these frameworks are able to inspire their teams, encourage new ideas, and create an environment where innovation can thrive. By utilizing Appreciative Inquiry and Integral Theory, leaders can tap into the full potential of their teams and drive positive change within their organization.

Utilizing Appreciative Inquiry and Integral Theory for

organizational change is another key aspect of fostering a culture of creativity and innovation. By focusing on strengths, possibilities, and positive outcomes, companies can create a shift in mindset that empowers employees to think outside the box and come up with innovative solutions to challenges. This approach to change management can lead to increased productivity, improved morale, and a greater sense of purpose within the organization.

Applying Appreciative Inquiry and Integral Theory for team building is crucial for creating a culture of creativity and innovation. By fostering a sense of collaboration, trust, and openness within teams, companies can create an environment where ideas can flow freely and innovation can flourish. By incorporating these frameworks into team building activities, companies can create a strong foundation for creativity and innovation to thrive.

Integrating Appreciative Inquiry and Integral Theory for cultural transformation is essential for companies looking to foster a culture of creativity and innovation. By aligning the values, beliefs, and behaviors of employees with the organization's goals and objectives, companies can create a culture that supports creativity, innovation, and growth. By incorporating these frameworks into cultural transformation efforts, companies can create a workplace where employees feel empowered to take risks, think creatively, and drive innovation forward.

Encouraging Risk-taking and Experimentation with Positive Inquiry

Encouraging risk-taking and experimentation with positive inquiry is a crucial aspect of fostering innovation and growth within corporations. By combining Appreciative Inquiry and Integral Theory, corporate executives can create a transformational framework that empowers employees to step outside their comfort zones and explore new possibilities.

Appreciative Inquiry, with its focus on strengths and positive questioning, encourages individuals to take risks and experiment with new ideas. By highlighting what is already working well within the organization, employees feel supported in trying out innovative approaches without fear of failure. Integral Theory, on the other hand, provides a comprehensive framework for understanding the complex interplay of factors that influence decision-making and behavior, allowing executives to design strategies that promote a culture of experimentation.

In leadership development, using Appreciative Inquiry and Integral Theory can help executives cultivate a mindset of curiosity and openness to new possibilities. By encouraging leaders to take risks and try out different approaches, organizations can foster a culture of continuous learning and improvement. This approach not only benefits individual leaders but also has a ripple effect throughout the entire organization, inspiring employees at all levels to embrace change and innovation.

When it comes to organizational change, Appreciative Inquiry and Integral Theory offer a powerful toolkit for driving transformation. By engaging employees in positive inquiry and encouraging them to experiment with new ways of working, organizations can adapt more easily to changing market conditions and technological advancements. This approach enables companies to stay ahead of the curve and remain competitive in today's fast-paced business environment.

In team building, integrating Appreciative Inquiry and Integral Theory can help executives create cohesive and high-performing teams. By fostering a culture of psychological safety and encouraging open communication, leaders can empower team members to take risks and collaborate on innovative solutions. This approach not only enhances team dynamics but also boosts productivity and creativity, leading to better outcomes for the organization as a whole.

Overall, by leveraging Appreciative Inquiry and Integral Theory in various aspects of corporate operations, executives can create a culture that values experimentation, risk-taking, and continuous improvement. By encouraging employees to step outside their comfort zones and explore new possibilities, organizations can drive innovation, enhance performance, and achieve sustainable growth in today's dynamic business landscape.

Using Integral Theory to Drive Innovation

In today's fast-paced business environment, innovation is key to staying ahead of the competition and driving growth. Corporate executives are constantly challenged to find new ways to innovate and adapt to changing market dynamics. One powerful framework that can help drive innovation within organizations is Integral Theory.

Integral Theory is a comprehensive framework that looks at the multiple dimensions of human experience and organizational dynamics. By understanding and integrating these dimensions, corporate executives can gain a holistic view of their organization and identify new opportunities for innovation. This framework helps leaders see the big picture and make connections between seemingly unrelated factors, leading to breakthrough ideas and solutions.

When combined with Appreciative Inquiry, Integral Theory becomes even more powerful. Appreciative Inquiry is a positive approach to organizational change that focuses on building on strengths and successes rather than fixing problems. By using Appreciative Inquiry in conjunction with Integral Theory, corporate executives can create a culture of innovation that values creativity, collaboration, and continuous improvement.

One way to utilize Appreciative Inquiry and Integral Theory for innovation is through leadership development. By fostering a culture of learning and growth, executives can empower their teams to think outside the box and experiment with new ideas. This approach encourages risk-taking and creativity, leading to breakthrough innovations that drive business success.

Another way to drive innovation using Appreciative Inquiry and Integral Theory is through organizational change. By involving employees at all levels in the change process and focusing on strengths and successes, executives can create a culture of innovation that embraces change and adapts to new opportunities. This approach helps organizations stay agile and responsive in a rapidly changing market.

In conclusion, using Appreciative Inquiry and Integral Theory to drive innovation can help corporate executives unlock the full potential of their organizations. By fostering a culture of creativity, collaboration, and continuous improvement, leaders can inspire their teams to think outside the box and generate breakthrough ideas. By integrating these powerful frameworks into their strategic planning, communication, and conflict resolution processes, executives can create a culture of innovation that drives business success and growth.

CHAPTER 10: LEVERAGING APPRECIATIVE INQUIRY AND INTEGRAL THEORY FOR CONFLICT RESOLUTION

Resolving Conflicts Peacefully and Positively

In the fast-paced and competitive world of corporate business, conflicts are inevitable. However, how these conflicts are resolved can make all the difference in the success of a company. By utilizing the powerful combination of Appreciative Inquiry and Integral Theory, corporate executives can learn to resolve conflicts peacefully and positively, fostering a more harmonious and productive work environment.

Appreciative Inquiry is a strength-based approach to organizational development that focuses on what is working well within a company, rather than dwelling on its weaknesses. Integral Theory, on the other hand, provides a comprehensive framework for understanding and addressing complex issues within an organization. By combining these two approaches, corporate executives can effectively address conflicts in a holistic and positive manner.

One key aspect of resolving conflicts peacefully and positively is through effective leadership development. By utilizing Appreciative Inquiry and Integral Theory in leadership development programs, executives can cultivate the skills and mindset needed to navigate conflicts with grace and understanding. This not only helps in resolving conflicts, but also in preventing them from escalating in the first place.

Another important application of Appreciative Inquiry and Integral Theory is in organizational change. By using these frameworks to guide change initiatives, corporate executives can ensure that conflicts are addressed in a constructive and proactive manner. This can lead to smoother transitions and a more resilient and adaptable organization.

Team building is another area where Appreciative Inquiry and Integral Theory can be incredibly beneficial in resolving conflicts. By fostering a culture of collaboration and mutual respect, executives can create a strong foundation for effective conflict resolution within teams. This can lead to increased productivity, creativity, and overall team performance.

In conclusion, the combination of Appreciative Inquiry and Integral Theory offers a powerful and transformative framework for resolving conflicts peacefully and positively in the corporate world. By leveraging these approaches in leadership development, organizational change, team building, and cultural transformation, executives can create a more harmonious and successful work environment. By incorporating these frameworks into strategic planning, communication, innovation, and employee engagement, corporate executives can maximize their company's performance and ensure long-term success.

Mediating Disputes with Appreciative Inquiry

In the world of corporate leadership, disputes and conflicts are inevitable. However, how these disputes are mediated can make a significant impact on the overall success of the organization. This is where Appreciative Inquiry and Integral Theory come into play as powerful tools for mediating disputes in a positive and transformative way.

Appreciative Inquiry is a strengths-based approach to change that focuses on what is working well within an organization rather than dwelling on problems and weaknesses. Integral Theory, on the other hand, is a comprehensive framework that looks at the big picture and considers all aspects of a situation. When combined, these two approaches create a powerful transformational framework that can help corporate executives mediate disputes effectively.

One of the key benefits of using Appreciative Inquiry and Integral Theory for mediating disputes is that it encourages a positive and collaborative approach to conflict resolution. Instead of focusing on blame and negativity, this approach helps parties involved in a dispute to focus on their common goals and values. By shifting the focus away from the problem and towards the solution, conflicts can be resolved more quickly and with less animosity.

Furthermore, by utilizing Appreciative Inquiry and Integral Theory for mediating disputes, corporate executives can foster a culture of open communication and trust within their organizations. This approach encourages employees to share their perspectives and work together towards a common goal, leading to stronger relationships and a more cohesive team.

Additionally, by incorporating Appreciative Inquiry and Integral Theory into conflict resolution processes, corporate executives can create lasting and sustainable solutions to disputes. Rather than simply putting a band-aid on the problem, this approach helps organizations to address the root causes of conflicts and implement changes that will prevent similar issues from arising in the future.

In conclusion, mediating disputes with Appreciative Inquiry

and Integral Theory can lead to more positive outcomes for organizations. By fostering a collaborative and solution-focused approach to conflict resolution, corporate executives can create a culture of trust, communication, and innovation within their organizations. By leveraging the power of Appreciative Inquiry and Integral Theory, disputes can be transformed into opportunities for growth and positive change.

Utilizing Integral Theory for Conflict Transformation

In the fast-paced world of corporate environments, conflicts are inevitable. Whether they stem from differing opinions, competition for resources, or even personal clashes, conflicts can hinder productivity and create a toxic work environment. As corporate executives, it is essential to have effective tools and strategies for conflict transformation. One powerful approach that has been gaining traction in recent years is the utilization of Integral Theory for conflict resolution.

Integral Theory is a comprehensive framework that considers multiple perspectives and dimensions of a situation. It acknowledges that conflicts are not simply black and white, but rather complex and multifaceted. By incorporating Integral Theory into conflict transformation processes, corporate executives can gain a deeper understanding of the root causes of conflicts and identify holistic solutions that address all aspects of the issue.

When combined with Appreciative Inquiry, another transformational framework that focuses on building on strengths and positive aspects of a situation, Integral Theory becomes even more potent. Appreciative Inquiry helps shift the focus from problems to possibilities, creating a positive and collaborative atmosphere for resolving conflicts. By utilizing both Appreciative Inquiry and Integral Theory, corporate executives can foster a culture of open communication, empathy, and understanding within their organizations.

Leadership development is another area where Appreciative Inquiry and Integral Theory can have a profound impact. By integrating these frameworks into leadership training programs, executives can cultivate a new generation of leaders who are equipped with the skills and mindset needed to effectively navigate conflicts and drive organizational success. Through a combination of self-awareness, emotional intelligence, and a deep understanding of integral perspectives, leaders can inspire their teams to work together harmoniously and achieve shared goals.

In conclusion, the integration of Appreciative Inquiry and Integral Theory offers a powerful transformational framework for conflict transformation in corporate settings. By leveraging the strengths of both approaches, corporate executives can enhance communication, foster collaboration, and resolve conflicts in a holistic and sustainable manner. As leaders strive to create thriving and innovative organizations, incorporating Appreciative Inquiry and Integral Theory into their conflict resolution strategies can pave the way for a more harmonious and productive work environment.

CHAPTER 11: MAXIMIZING PERFORMANCE WITH APPRECIATIVE INQUIRY AND INTEGRAL THEORY

Enhancing Individual and Team Performance

In the fast-paced and competitive world of corporate business, enhancing individual and team performance is crucial for success. By utilizing the powerful combination of Appreciative Inquiry and Integral Theory, corporate executives can unlock the full potential of their employees and teams. These transformational frameworks provide a holistic approach to leadership development, organizational change, team building, and cultural transformation.

Appreciative Inquiry and Integral Theory in Leadership Development focus on developing leaders who are not only effective in achieving goals but also inspire and motivate their teams. By incorporating principles of positive psychology and integral theory, leaders can create a supportive and inclusive work environment that fosters growth and innovation.

Utilizing Appreciative Inquiry and Integral Theory for

Organizational Change enables executives to navigate complex challenges and adapt to changing market conditions. By focusing on strengths and possibilities rather than weaknesses and problems, organizations can effectively manage change and overcome obstacles with resilience and creativity.

Applying Appreciative Inquiry and Integral Theory for Team Building emphasizes the importance of collaboration, trust, and communication within teams. By encouraging open dialogue, sharing of ideas, and valuing diverse perspectives, teams can work together cohesively towards common goals and achieve outstanding results.

Integrating Appreciative Inquiry and Integral Theory for Cultural Transformation involves aligning organizational values, beliefs, and practices with a shared vision of success. By fostering a culture of appreciation, inclusivity, and continuous improvement, companies can create a positive and engaging work environment that motivates employees to perform at their best. Through these transformative frameworks, corporate executives can enhance individual and team performance, maximize employee engagement, and drive innovation and success in their organizations.

Setting Performance Goals with Positive Inquiry

Setting performance goals with positive inquiry is a crucial aspect of corporate success. By utilizing the power of Appreciative Inquiry and Integral Theory, corporate executives can create a transformational framework that not only enhances individual and team performance but also drives organizational change and cultural transformation. This subchapter will explore how the combination of Appreciative Inquiry and Integral Theory can be leveraged to set meaningful and achievable performance goals that inspire and motivate employees to reach their full potential.

In leadership development, Appreciative Inquiry and Integral Theory provide a unique approach to setting performance goals that focuses on strengths and possibilities rather than weaknesses and limitations. By using positive inquiry techniques, leaders can empower their teams to identify their unique talents and capabilities, leading to more effective goal-setting and performance management. This approach not only boosts employee engagement but also fosters a culture of continuous learning and growth within the organization.

When it comes to organizational change, Appreciative Inquiry and Integral Theory offer a powerful framework for setting performance goals that align with the company's vision and values. By involving employees in the goal-setting process and encouraging them to focus on positive outcomes, organizations can drive meaningful change that leads to sustainable growth and success. This approach also helps to build trust and collaboration among team members, creating a more cohesive and productive work environment.

In team building, Appreciative Inquiry and Integral Theory can be used to set performance goals that promote synergy and collaboration among team members. By focusing on strengths and shared values, teams can work together more effectively towards common objectives, leading to improved communication, productivity, and morale. This approach also helps to build a strong sense of team identity and purpose, fostering a culture of mutual support and accountability within the organization.

In conclusion, setting performance goals with positive inquiry using Appreciative Inquiry and Integral Theory is key to maximizing performance, enhancing communication, and driving innovation within organizations. By incorporating these powerful frameworks into strategic planning, leadership development, and organizational change initiatives, corporate executives can create a culture of continuous improvement and excellence that propels their companies to new heights of success.

Monitoring and Evaluating Performance using Integral

Theory

Monitoring and evaluating performance is a crucial aspect of corporate success, as it allows organizations to track progress, identify areas for improvement, and make data-driven decisions. When it comes to utilizing Integral Theory in this process, it provides a comprehensive framework that considers all aspects of an organization's performance, including individual, team, and organizational levels.

Integral Theory, developed by philosopher Ken Wilber, is based on the idea that reality is composed of multiple dimensions or perspectives, and that a holistic approach is necessary to fully understand and address complex issues. When applied to monitoring and evaluating performance, Integral Theory helps corporate executives consider not just financial metrics, but also factors such as employee engagement, cultural dynamics, and strategic alignment.

By combining Integral Theory with Appreciative Inquiry, a positive and strengths-based approach to organizational development, corporate executives can create a powerful framework for transformation. Appreciative Inquiry focuses on what is working well within an organization and seeks to amplify those strengths, rather than focusing solely on fixing problems. When used in conjunction with Integral Theory, this approach can help organizations achieve sustainable performance improvements by leveraging their existing strengths and resources.

When monitoring and evaluating performance using Integral Theory and Appreciative Inquiry, it's important for corporate executives to engage all stakeholders in the process. This can help ensure that diverse perspectives are considered, and that the evaluation is comprehensive and inclusive. By involving employees, customers, and other key stakeholders in the monitoring and evaluation process, organizations can gain valuable insights and create a more accurate picture of their performance.

Ultimately, by incorporating Integral Theory and Appreciative Inquiry into the monitoring and evaluation process, corporate executives can create a more holistic and effective approach to performance management. This framework allows organizations to not only track financial metrics, but also consider factors such as employee engagement, organizational culture, and strategic alignment. By leveraging the strengths of both Integral Theory and Appreciative Inquiry, corporate executives can drive meaningful and sustainable performance improvements that lead to long-term success.

CONCLUSION: THE FUTURE OF CORPORATE TRANSFORMATION WITH APPRECIATIVE INQUIRY AND INTEGRAL THEORY

In conclusion, the future of corporate transformation lies in the integration of Appreciative Inquiry and Integral Theory. This powerful combination offers a holistic approach to organizational change and development, allowing corporate executives to tap into the full potential of their teams and organizations. By leveraging the strengths of both frameworks, companies can create a culture of positivity, collaboration, and innovation that drives success in today's fast-paced business environment.

One of the key benefits of using Appreciative Inquiry and Integral Theory in leadership development is the focus on strengths and possibilities rather than weaknesses and problems. This approach empowers leaders to inspire their teams and cultivate a shared vision for the future. By incorporating these frameworks into leadership training programs, companies can develop a new generation of leaders who are equipped to navigate complex challenges and drive lasting change.

When it comes to organizational change, Appreciative Inquiry and Integral Theory offer a unique perspective that focuses on the interconnectedness of all aspects of a company. By utilizing these frameworks, executives can identify areas for improvement, develop strategic plans for change, and engage employees in the transformation process. This results in a more agile and resilient organization that is better equipped to adapt to changing market conditions and seize new opportunities.

Team building is another area where Appreciative Inquiry and Integral Theory can make a significant impact. By fostering a culture of collaboration, trust, and open communication, companies can create high-performing teams that drive innovation and achieve results. Integrating these frameworks into team building initiatives can help executives build cohesive and motivated teams that are aligned with the organization's goals and values.

In conclusion, the future of corporate transformation with Appreciative Inquiry and Integral Theory is bright. By integrating these frameworks into every aspect of their business, executives can create a culture of positivity, collaboration, and innovation that drives success. Whether it's leadership development, organizational change, team building, or cultural transformation, Appreciative Inquiry and Integral Theory offer a powerful toolkit for driving lasting change and achieving corporate success.

www.ingramcontent.com/pod-product-compliance
Lightning Source LLC
Chambersburg PA
CBHW070127230526
45472CB00004B/1458

9 7 9 8 3 2 8 0 1 3 4 3 7